Plum Village
An Artist's Journey

Plum Village
An Artist's Journey

**FINDING INNER PEACE AT
THICH NHAT HANH'S BUDDHIST MONASTERY**

PHAP BAN

FOREWORD BY ALEJANDRO G. IÑÁRRITU

Originally published as *Plum Village Love Story*

MANDALA
PUBLISHING
San Rafael, California

FOREWORD

In the summer of 2012, under the shade of an oak tree in Plum Village, fourteen Spanish-speakers waited eagerly to meet the monk who had been assigned to them for the twenty-one-day meditation retreat "Buddhism and Quantum Physics," commanded by Master Thich Nhat Hanh, also called Thay.

It was my first day on retreat in my life, and the heat and humidity accentuated my feelings of curiosity, reserve, and anxiety.

After a few words of introduction, our assigned monk made this request: "I ask you not to be enlightened on the first or second day, because then what are you going to do next?"

With a soft voice and a natural smile, the monk, Phap Ban, opened with a sense of humor that made my expectations of solemnity on his part vanish. Phap Ban is Italian, but his Spanish is very clear.

The goal he assigned us during the first week was to rest and sleep as much as our bodies asked of us. In addition to meditation sessions at 5:00 a.m., Thay's talks at noon, and meditation again at nightfall, another important part of the retreat was the meeting (or therapy) with the Spanish-speaking family under the oak tree, moderated by Phap Ban.

During these group sessions, hearts opened up, painful memories arose, and the uncertainties, anxieties, and unanswered questions of each one of us floated under the foliage of the tree. Only occasionally, and with extreme prudence and sweetness, would Phap Ban comment or offer a reflection that seemed to point us back to meditation, without ever trying to give a solution.

Phap Ban lived in a tiny wood house in the middle of the forest inside Plum Village. One day, he invited me to visit him and he showed me his drawings. His long, skilled, pianist's fingers were able to trace deep human emotions in an immediate and intuitive manner suitable for dreams and memories. His drawings and stories transcended intuition because there was a foundation beneath them. Phap Ban began his career as a cartoonist at Disney Studios in Italy, and I realized that his talent was not improvised. It was delightful seeing a Buddhist monk with his long brown robes drawing wonderful lines and colors on an iPad with such fluency and command of the technology. Phap Ban departs from the material, the explicit, and the artisanal to reach the mystery of the immaterial and the implicit, which is nothing but consciousness.

Consciousness is a personal experience. Nevertheless, when one is in the presence of a conscious being, an enlightened being, something is implicit in that person and can be felt but can never be explained. That is the feeling one has being with Phap Ban.

Claudio, which is his first name, plays guitar, composes songs, secretly cooks the best spaghetti (especially after weeks of only vegetables while in retreat), and sings with the same grace and dedication with which he draws, meditates, and enlightens whoever is near him. Over the years, Phap Ban has helped to keep the tiny flame of consciousness alive in each one of the members of the oak tree family who had the privilege of participating in that Plum Village retreat with Thay. Since then, my life has been impacted and transformed forever. Once you grasp the juices of consciousness even a little bit, there is no turning back. The Knower (you) starts observing the Thinker (your mind) and a whole new knowledge and relationship is established. It triggers an infinite curiosity, to which Buddhist monks devote their whole life. As I have explained to my kids, I was an iPhone 3 looking for an upgrade, and Claudio, an engineer and iPhone 12, showed me some new apps that helped me navigate and communicate with myself more clearly.

The spiritual awakening of each person is so precious and fragile that, when it's described, it runs the risk of being trapped in an anecdote and losing its flight, like a butterfly exposed lifeless in a case. However, the complex transformation of a human being from an ordinary man to an artist to a Buddhist monk remains alive in this beautiful love story, thanks to the simplicity, honesty, and innocence with which Phap Ban tells and illustrates it.

Phap Ban found his spiritual awakening by following the path initiated by Thich Nhat Hanh. In describing that loving encounter with the mission and vision of the great Master Thay, Phap Ban shares with us his intimate experience of the eternal possibility within each of us—to abandon ourselves to love and consciousness as the greatest conquest of ourselves.

Alejandro G. Iñárritu
Oscar-winning director of *Birdman* and *The Revenant*

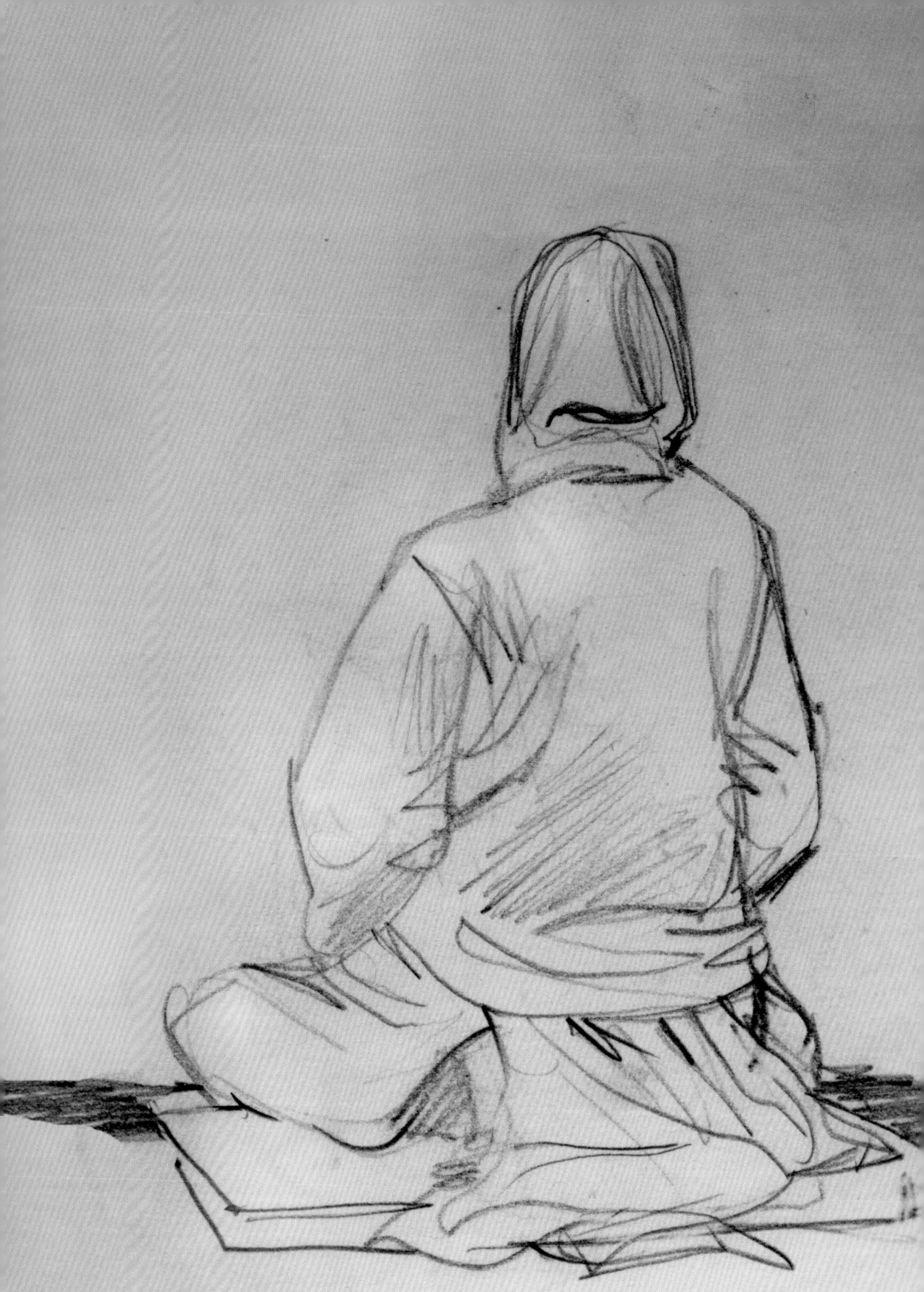

INTRODUCTION

If there were an explanation for everything in the world,
that would be a good complaint.

Natalia Ginzburg

We are all superheroes,
each one with their own superpower,
each one with their green kryptonite.

Peter Pankov

These two stories were born in 2011, when Thay—the name we affectionately use for our Master Thich Nhat Hanh—asked us, at the end of one of his dharma teachings, to tell the story of our love for Plum Village with photos, poetry, videos, or narratives.

Plum Village is our monastery in France, founded by Thay in 1982, and it is also, by extension, all the other monasteries that have since been founded on its model all over the world.

Plum Village is the hundreds of monks and nuns coming from all over the world who were ordained by Thay, little by little. It is the laypeople that live there and it is those who have come to live in the outskirts of the monastery.

Plum Village is the thousands of people—atheists, Christians, Jews, or Muslims—who, without any affiliations or sectarianism, come for a few days, alone or with their families. They don't come to practice an exotic religion or learn about a new philosophy but to immerse themselves in life, to explore together the mystery of happiness and of suffering. Children are often the ones who never want to leave.

Above all, Plum Village is Thay and his teachings, his wisdom, and his tenderness. Those who have not met him might think of this affection we have for him as a form of idolatry, but Thay is an open window to the mystery of life. Just watching him walk, then pour and drink some tea, brings out a natural respect in the observer. His very presence is an invitation to try the way of the breath and of silence.

It came naturally to me to tell of my love for Plum Village through images. For me this story was both an opportunity for spiritual nourishment and a form of dialogue with Thay and with my monastic brothers and sisters. We are all united by a sort of Anglo-Esperanto, a kind of slang worthy of the Tower of Babel. This does not prevent us from understanding each other, even when language fails us from time to time.

This is the story of a "lazy" morning. At the monastery we have a "lazy day" each week. On that day, besides tending to our daily tasks of cooking and taking care of the pots and of the bell, we don't follow our usual tight schedule and our practice is informal.

Thay had told us of a Vietnamese woman who had kept her husband's love letters in a tin box. During a difficult time in their marriage, she had reread them. Since I seemed unable to get out of bed that heavy morning, I began to recall my arrival at Plum Village twenty years earlier—the enthusiasm of the discovery, the fruits of meditation—and began to write my own love letter.

I arrived at Plum Village in 1992. I was in my early thirties and was with my friend Paolo, with whom I had discovered Thay, thanks to a book, a few years before.

Had the book's title been *Introduction to Buddhism,* I never would have read it. The only so-called Buddhists I knew at that time were a bunch of smart alecks, slightly nerdy, with dark circles under their eyes.

I used to fear religions and would look at them with distrust. Spirituality in general seemed to me something for counterrevolutionary freaks, for spiritualists and UFO trackers. My goodness . . . it's amazing to think of how many ideas can change in one's lifetime, and the funny thing is that there is only one thing that always stays the same: the absolute certainty of being right!

Fortunately, the title of the book was *Introduction to Zen,* and you know, *Zen* sounds much cooler than *Buddhism.* You immediately conjure the image of a slow-moving, superpatient individual, clothed in a black robe ragged at the hemlines. Someone who always gives you the right answer and perhaps even gets you to laugh or, worse comes to worst, wakes you up by hitting you with a bamboo stick.

I remember reading that fateful book, full of drawings and incomprehensible koans. Yet, despite having understood none of it, I had found it! I had found what I was looking for. And in that moment, I realized I had been looking for it, and how ardently. It was like turning around and looking back. I had looked for it everywhere: in my philosophy and psychology studies; in the many books I devoured; in anything that had a scent of truth, of authenticity; in the attempt of merging into love; in wild discussions with friends in the heart of the night. And now I had found it.

And maybe that's the way some important encounters in our life are: It's like finding each other again. I remember Paolo's look when we met up after we had both read the book. That silence, that hesitation just before sharing our enthusiasm. We had both found what we were looking for.

Then, the dive into reading about Zen. A new way of reading, a spacious one, a way of reading with the body as well.

Thay came to Italy in 1992. That summer, we were on a train headed to France, the same one I later took dozens and dozens of times. Usually people approach meditation during a difficult time in their life, after searching for happiness in every possible direction. Then when there is nothing else left, they try meditation, thinking who knows . . . There's nothing wrong with that, but at the time I tried meditation, everything was going strangely well: Finally, I had a job at Disney and I had just started living with my beloved. I was in love, surrounded by friends, with a nice home and my own studio. For the last few years I had been on a rich path of personal and group bioengergetics practice. There I discovered dynamic meditation and above all, finally, a new relationship with my body. Yet I sensed—somewhat consciously—an anxiety, a restlessness that was constantly with me. I only later purged it.

The sudden, unexpected decision to become a monk, the years spent as a layman at Plum Village, the resistance, and, finally, the moment I became an aspirant; the initial ordination, the novitiate, the complete ordination; then my father's death and the great gift from my brothers of being able to continue the monastic life in Italy. Moving through contradictions, incongruences, and one obvious choice: staying on the path. My journey hasn't always been simple.

It takes a lot of courage to be happy.

Plum Village is my love, and like a great love, we have gone through ups and downs: falling in love, engagement, marriage, separation, rekindling passion, and friendship. Like any other great love, it is an opportunity to know oneself more deeply, to recognize and let go of useless attachments, engrained ideas, opinions, defenses.

My grandmother used to ride the bus for a free tour with her girlfriends. The bus would be packed with elderly women and would cross the entire Liguria region and the French Riviera, stopping in a dozen different places. Inevitably, at the end of the day while on the way back, they would be shown some very expensive stainless steel cookware with fantastic powers like those of a Transformer or a Mazinger, which were so popular on TV in those very days. Some of those pots happily got me through more than a few dinners in my little bare house during my student years.

What I tried to avoid doing with this book was selling pots; I didn't want to become a salesman of spiritual goods. You see, in the spiritual world, there is a strong demand for a perfect world with no wrinkles, no contradictions, where you can take refuge to alleviate or even bypass the hardships, the compromises, the little daily sorrows.

Thus a story was born, perhaps not so "spiritually correct." I tried to bring back that sense of awe, of enthusiasm, of surprise, and at times of embarrassment that pervaded me when I crashed into this new world. I was not so much attracted by the notion of walking this path "together," much less of becoming "good," but by the burning desire for personal growth. I was driven by an underlying suffering that—in order to finally heal—needed to come out of the darkness from where it was directing my thoughts and actions.

Over the years, my motivation, my aspiration, naturally changed, or rather, broadened, in the slow discovery of the profound relationship between my own suffering-happiness and the suffering-happiness of others.

Now practicing with others makes me happy, and it is much easier.

Rereading these two stories, I confess I felt some shame for publicly exposing my dirty laundry, but also the clean laundry, those inspirational and pretentious phrases. I hope I did not give the impression of being some kind of teacher or somebody who really gets it.

In short, I did not understand anything, and not knowing is a beautiful and vast place where you don't have to do homework and can therefore rest.

I am not a master, not even a substitute teacher. At best, I am a nerd and not even one of the brightest ones. I am one of those nerds that the master leaves standing in front of the desk during a short absence. Fortunately, instead of writing the names of the good and bad kids on the board, I started drawing with the chalk.

Phap Ban
Salento, Puglia (Italy)

To my beloved Master Thay
with gratitude

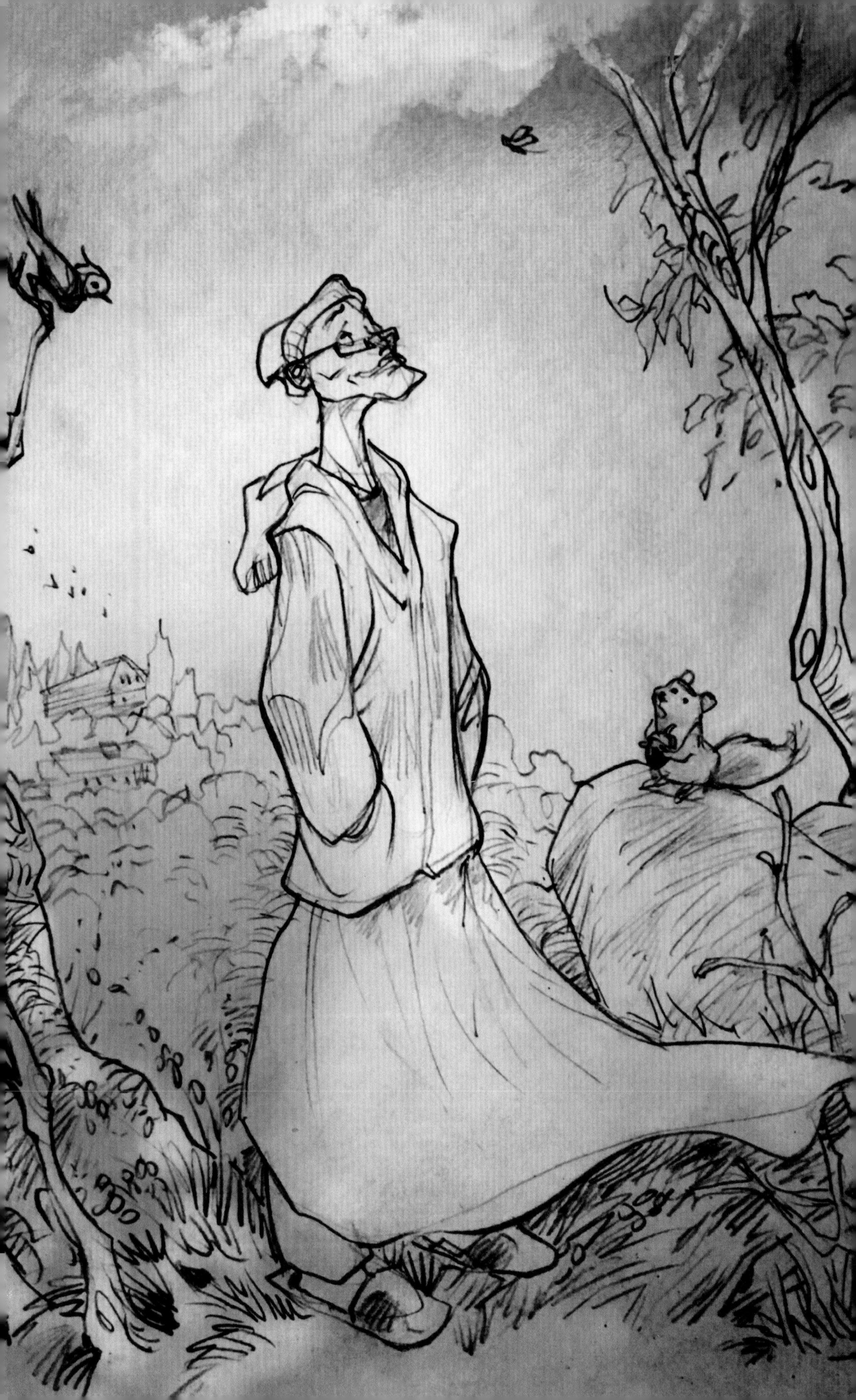

Part 1

20 Years Later

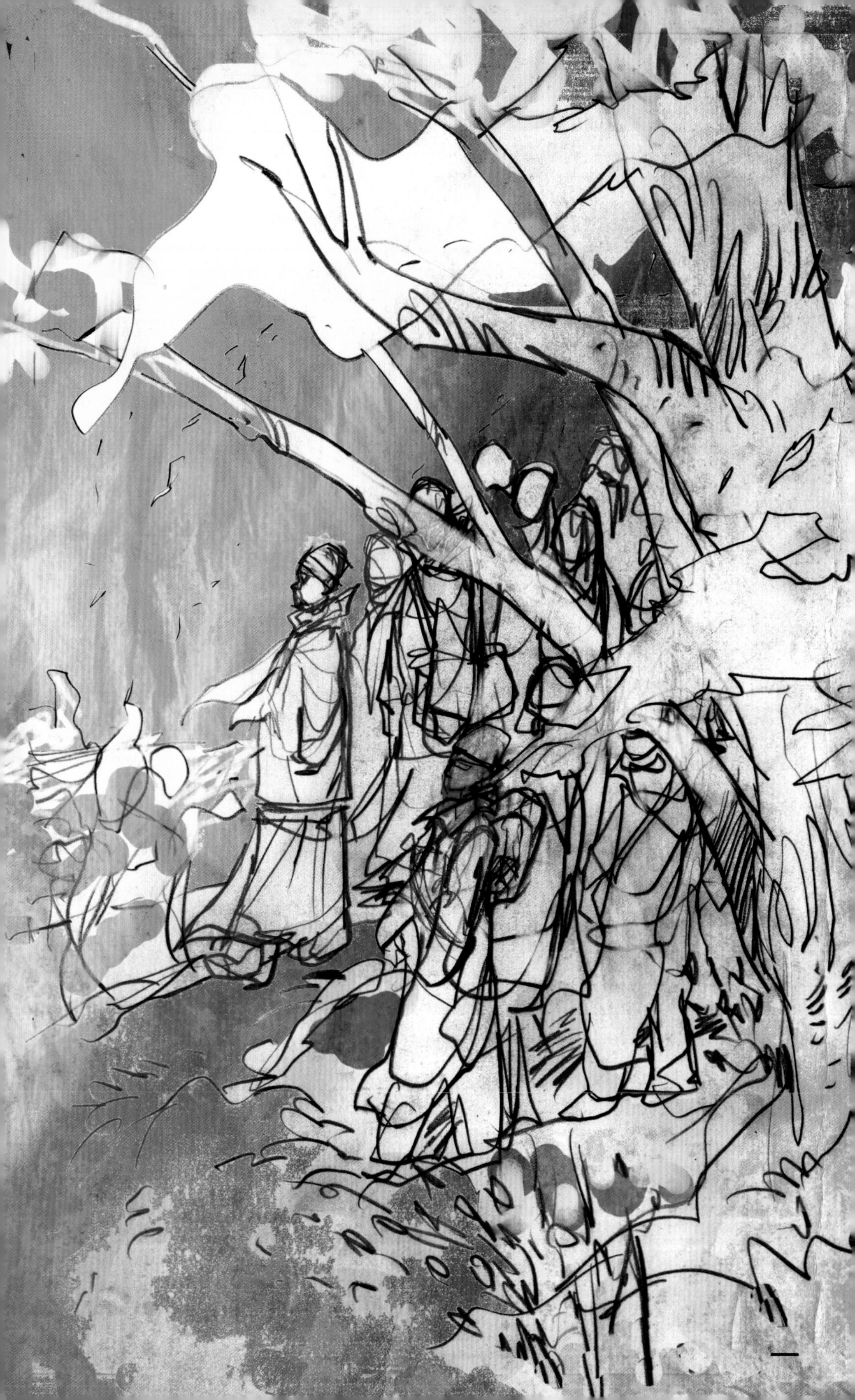

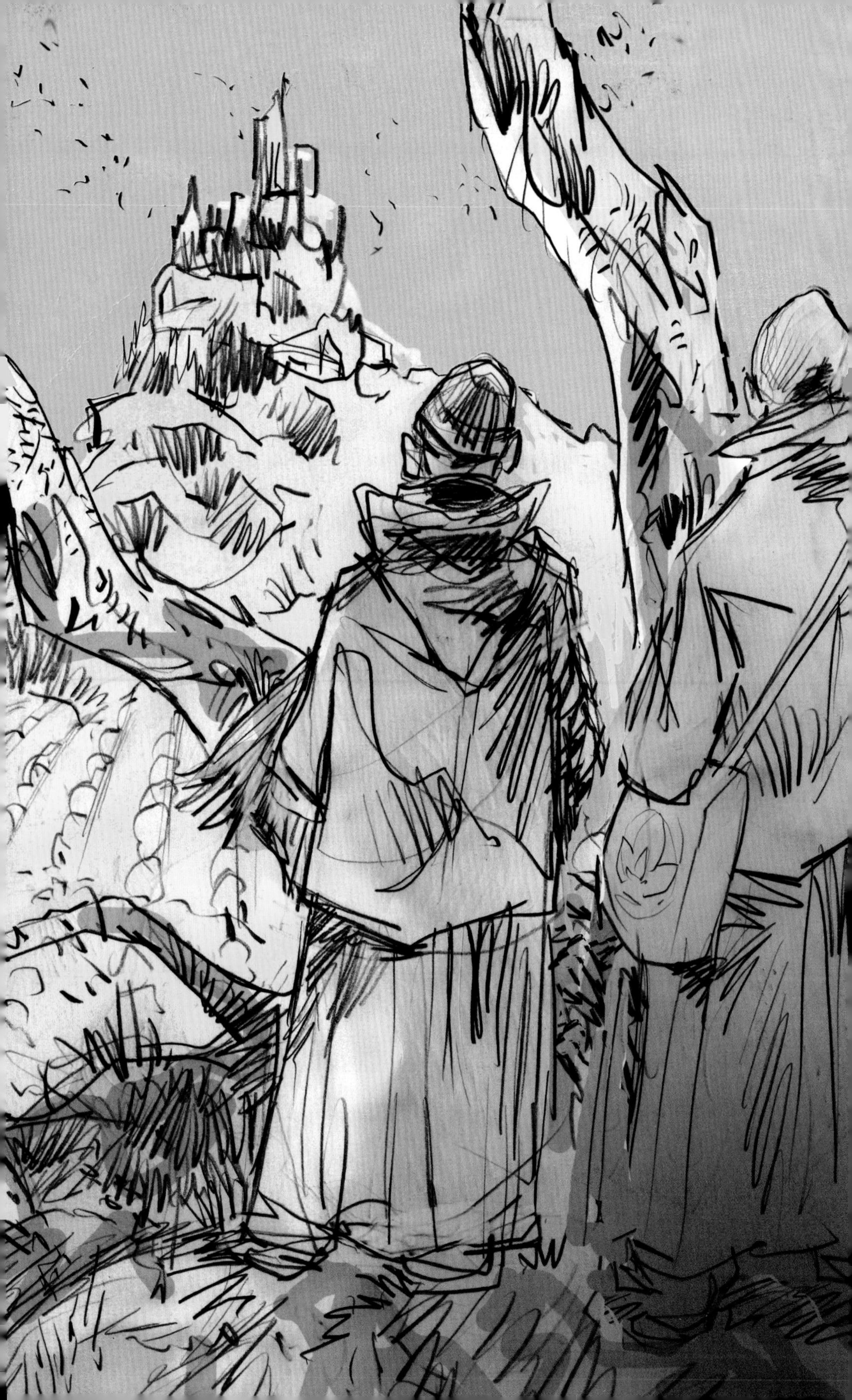

You are what you are looking for.
You are already what you want to become.
You can say to the wave,
"My dearest wave, you are water.
You don't have to go and seek water."

Thich Nhat Hanh

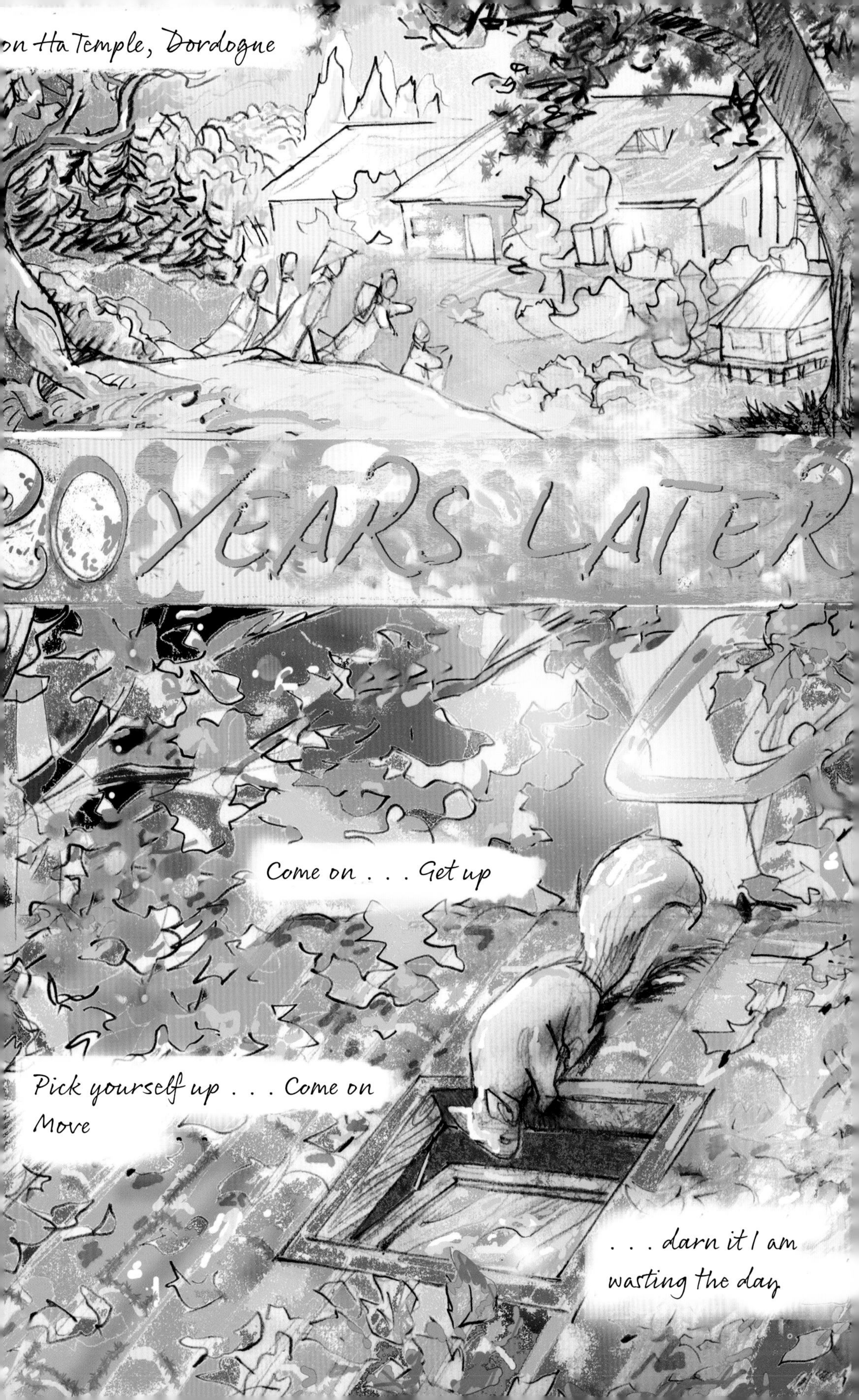
on Ha Temple, Dordogne
20 YEARS LATER
Come on . . . Get up
Pick yourself up . . . Come on
Move
. . . darn it I am
wasting the day

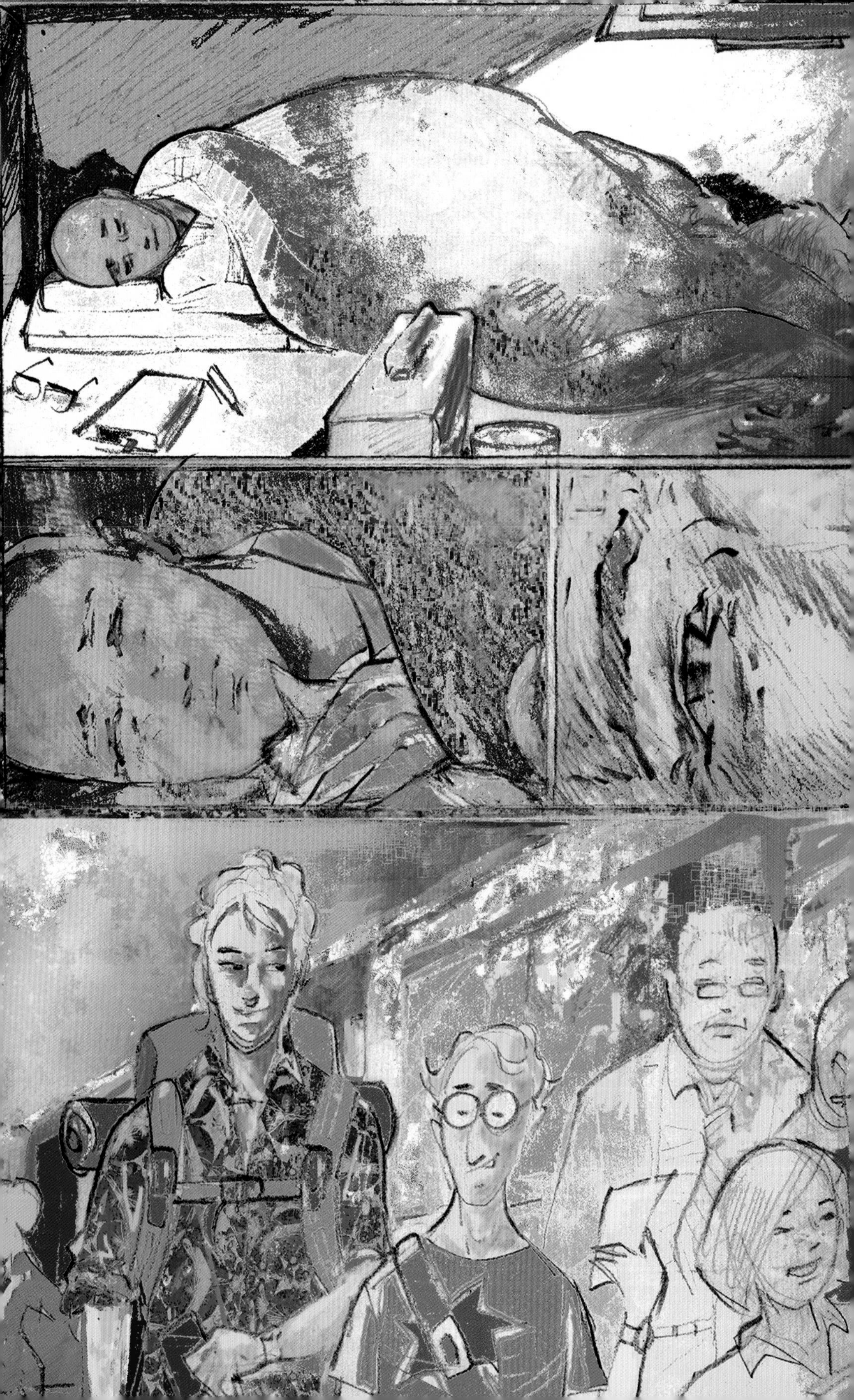

No way

I can't get up

I woke up here in the attic among abandoned
suitcases and old sewing machines
I came here so I could sleep a little longer
since this morning there is no meditation and . . .
I guess it wasn't such a good idea . . .

It feels like having a big fat elephant sitting
on my chest

and then I remember . . .

Twenty years ago
My first time here
The arrival in the little train station of Sainte–Foy
with my friend Paolo

Ten days spent in the monastery   Old stone houses
The warmth of the people   of the monks   of the nuns

The shame of singing in a circle like boy scouts
At times it felt like being at summer camp

Yet those chants hid eternal truths
Neither pure nor impure
Neither coming nor going
Neither before nor after . . .

the bell would stop the world   and
suddenly we'd be reminded
of something that we had always known

It seemed as if I had come home
A home that I had forgotten I had

Peace   contemplation   but also joy
there was even a ping-pong table

and the soccer game   rough and gentle
You could breathe the softness and the joy of being together

and then in front of the huge linden tree there was the meditation hall
an old stable with planed logs that fit together to support
the high ceiling   the old stone walls
the smell of incense mixed with the smoke from the stoves

behind the ticking of the clock
behind the sudden scream of a swallow

a vast river of silence would appear

meditation
what a small and complicated word for something so broad and simple
nothing to fix   nothing to cut off
                                        everything is accepted   breath...
maybe it's just the courage to feel and to rest in this intensity

And that little man saying things I had never heard before
absurd   yet so familiar

When, on the last day of the retreat, he would make
the simple gesture of lighting a match   in that gesture there
was the secret of life and death   like a grandfather that
tries to explain to his grandchild the movements of the stars

It's strange   but the thing that amazed me the most
        happened at the end of those ten summer days
in Bordeaux   wandering in the streets of the old city
waiting for the train that would bring us back to Genoa

Everything was so simple
bright   real

and so I began to sit

n minutes every morning
        with my cat by my side

my body still or almost   my mind racing between the past and
the future   totally uninterested in the present . . . Worries   projects
A powerful relentless stream of thoughts until the alarm struck
        I remember often asking myself what was the use of sitting there

And one morning while riding my little Vespa to work

among the tops of the sycamore trees I saw a tiny slice of the sky

A blue sky
            nothing special

        but enough to discover that something was happening

Something was slowly timidly growing
something that did not need any words
the many words of the books I used to read

it did not need to understand   to solve
            to heal

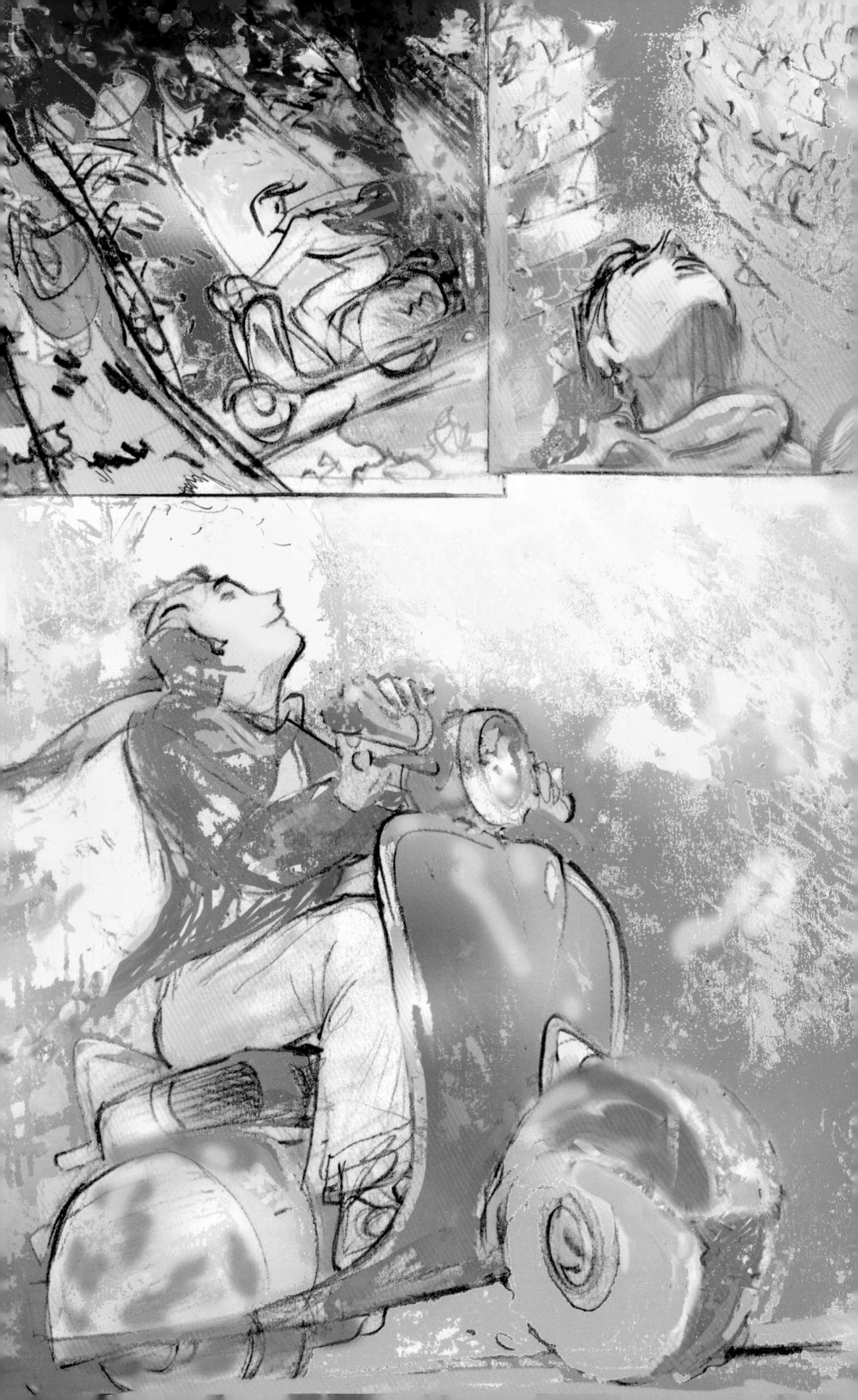

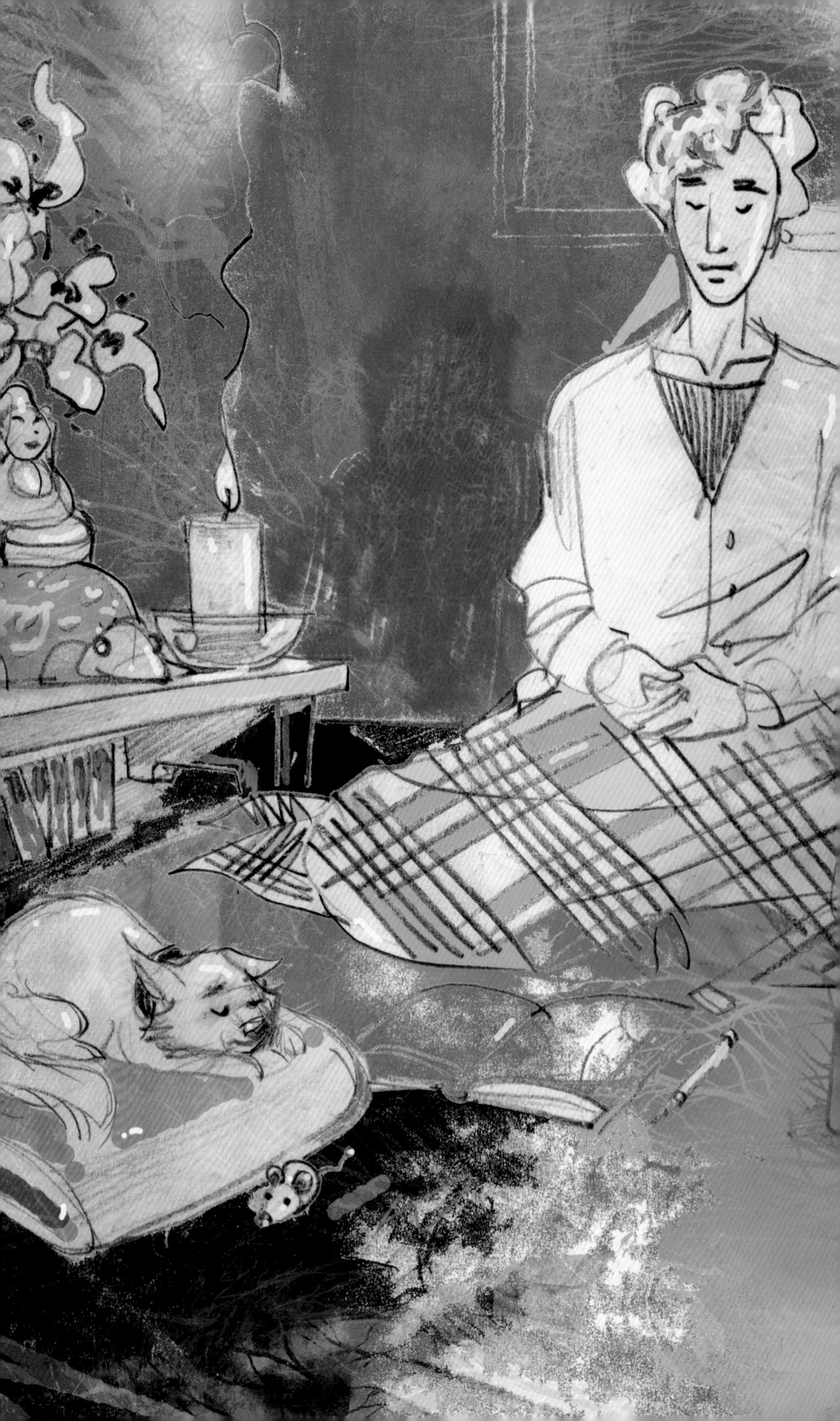

Only feeling   just feeling
the courage of letting go of the stories of the mind
and remembering to rest in that physical sensation

feel it   feel it   feel it

It was like entering a new world
strange   unusual but very beautiful
something that had to do
with reality   with life

the practice little by little invaded my life

like a great calm river

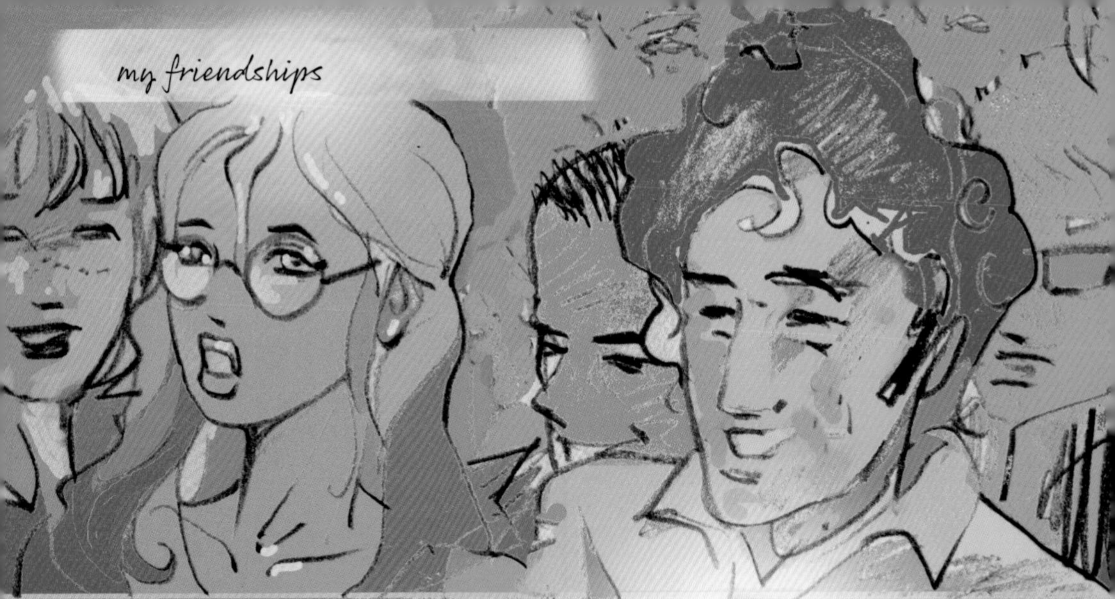
my friendships

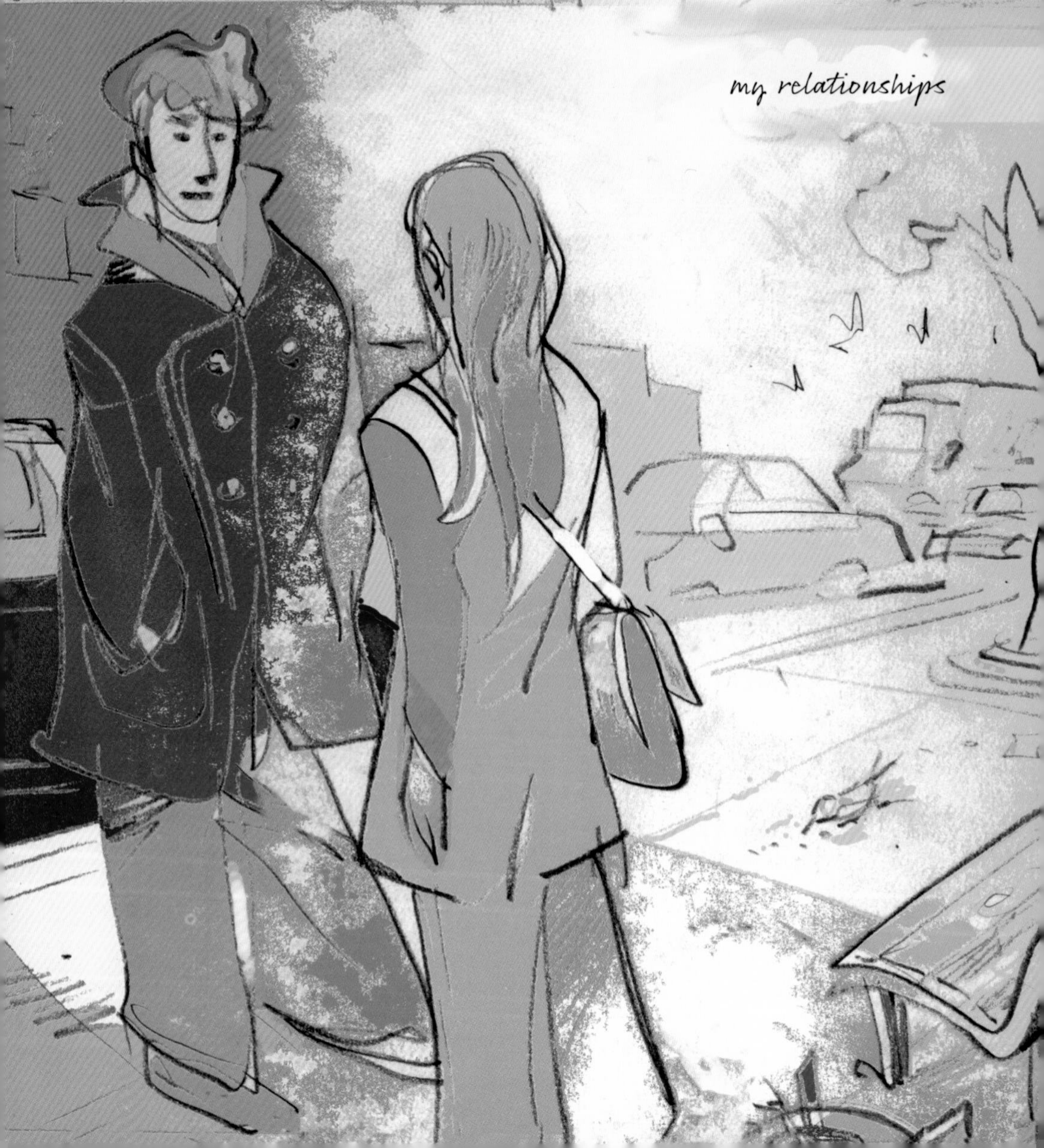
my relationships

my work

The Buddha of Donald Duck
does he have a beak?

Yes   I think so

Throughout the day suddenly
the images of the village would come to mind

the ecstatic joy of a nun who
taught me how to sit and breathe

the deep sound of the bell in the Zendo

the dancing of the light with the smoke from the incense
the silence

I would wake up smiling . . .

It had never happened before

Everything was simply perfect
Life was flowing with me

. the feeling of having understood everything
d so I started giving advice left and right

What a fool . . .

Jesus said that the "spiritual expert" is like
a dog that sleeps on the hay of a manger
It does not eat the hay, but at the same time it prevents
those who might be hungry from eating it

Life does not like arrogance

It calls you   it calls you again
It taps you on the shoulder   it pulls your jacket
and then a mighty blow strikes you

And it hurts

But my plaster Buddha
Kept riding the papier-mâché turtle . . .

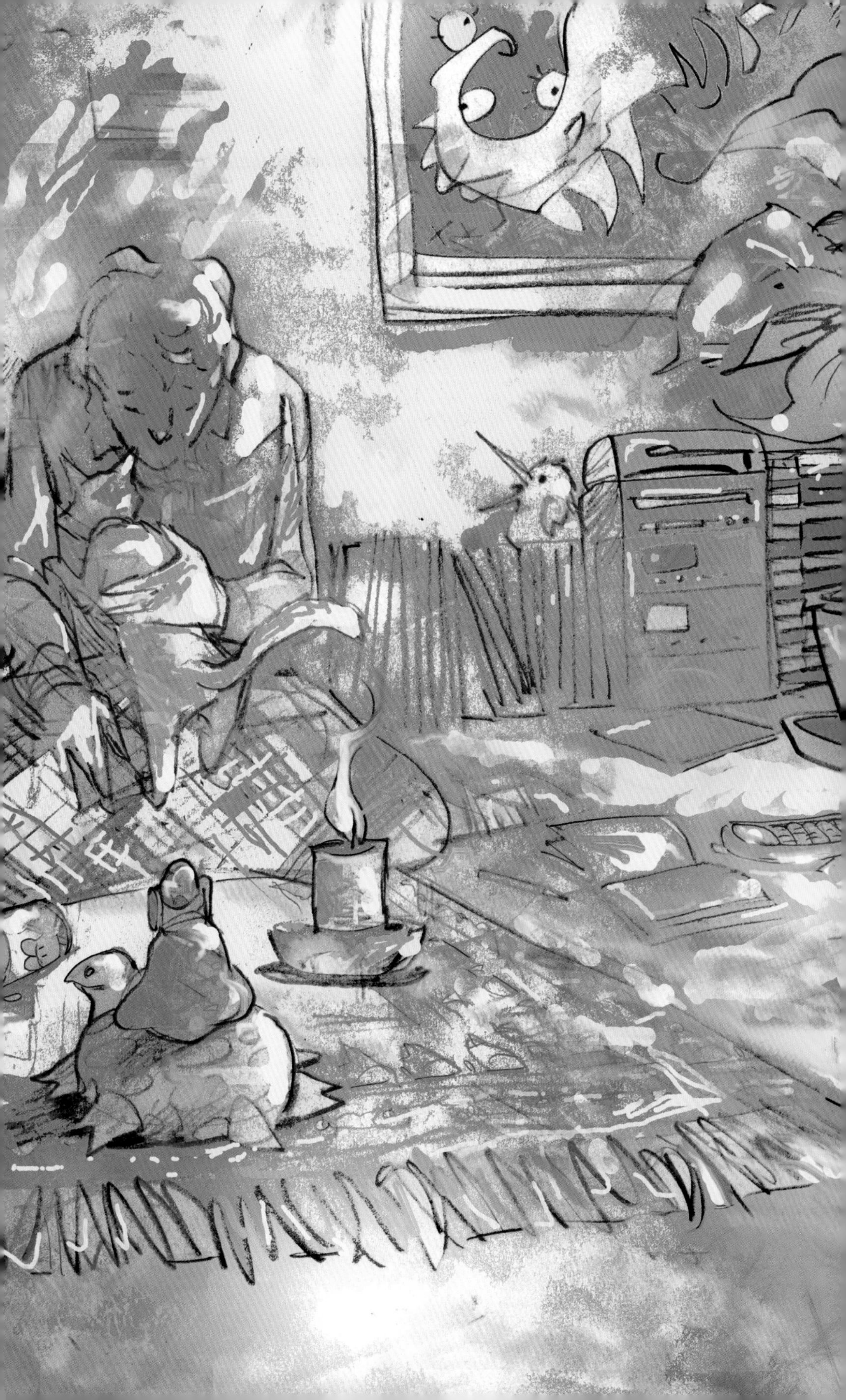

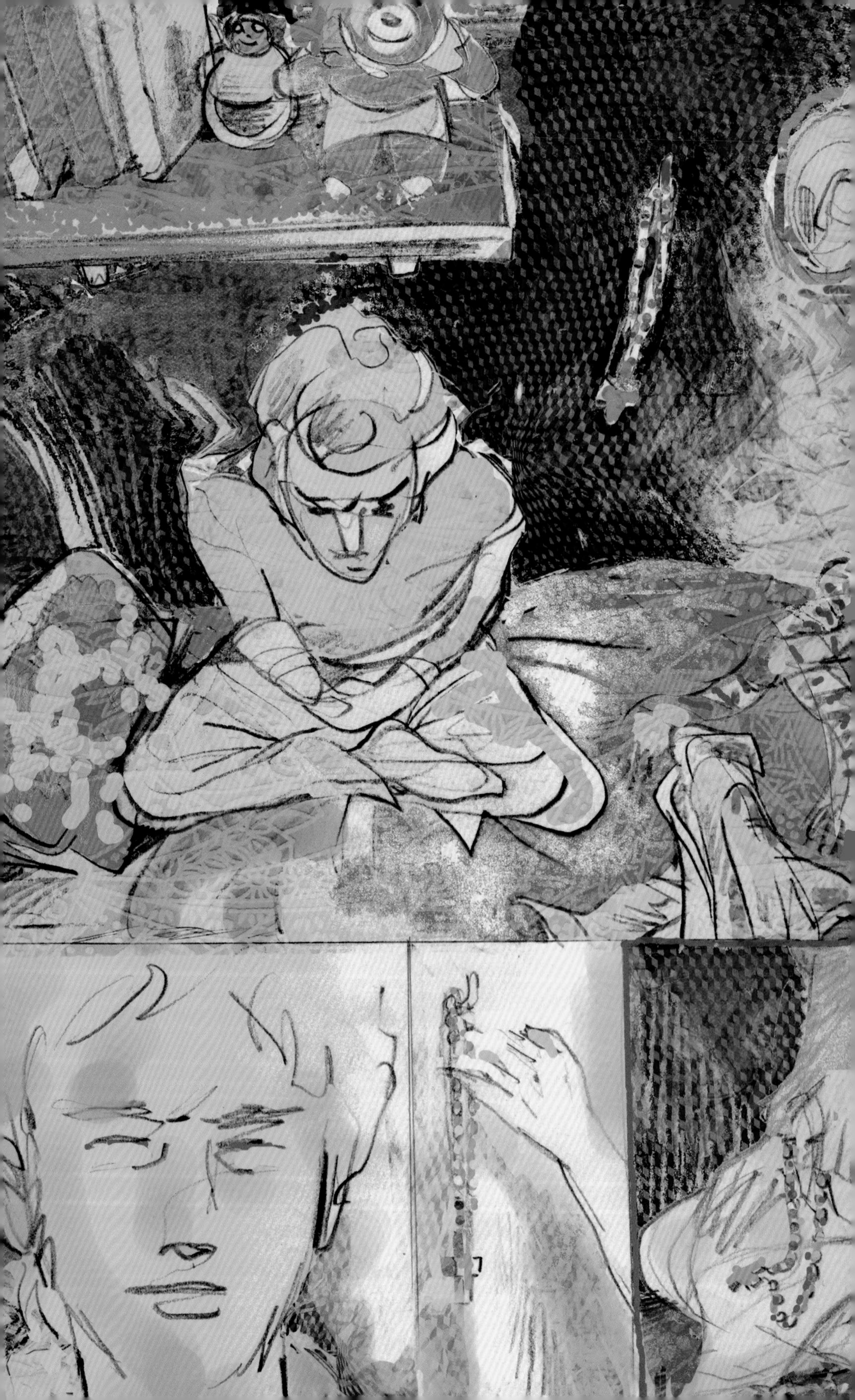

Going to Otranto with my sister to meet our father after many years
A few hours and we already wanted to take the plane to get back home

On the wall of the little rented room
A pink plastic rosary

One bead   I breathe in
One bead   I breathe out
One bead   my violence   immense
One bead   the immense violence of my father
One bead   in the heart of violence   fear
One bead   the boy terrified by his father
One bead   I am no longer a boy
One bead   I am free

At times it works

Just like in the books

At times life gives you what you want
At times it does what it wants and gives you something different

This path is a good path
I am a little jealous from time to time
but it's a good path

He who seeks, let him not cease seeking until he finds;
and when he finds he will be troubled,
and when he is troubled he will be amazed,
and he will reign over the All.

Gospel of Thomas

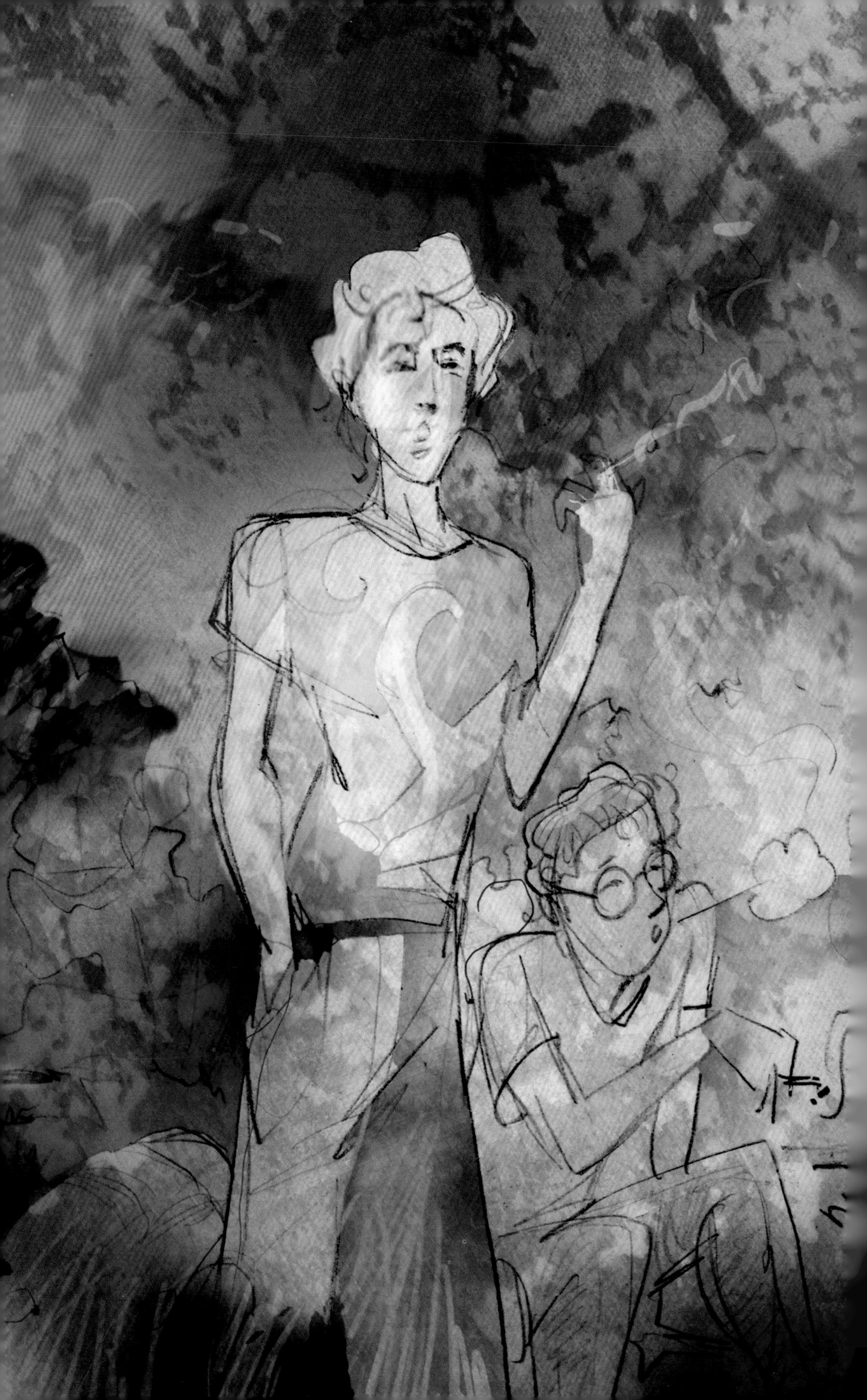

For those two young men
and for all those who are seeking.

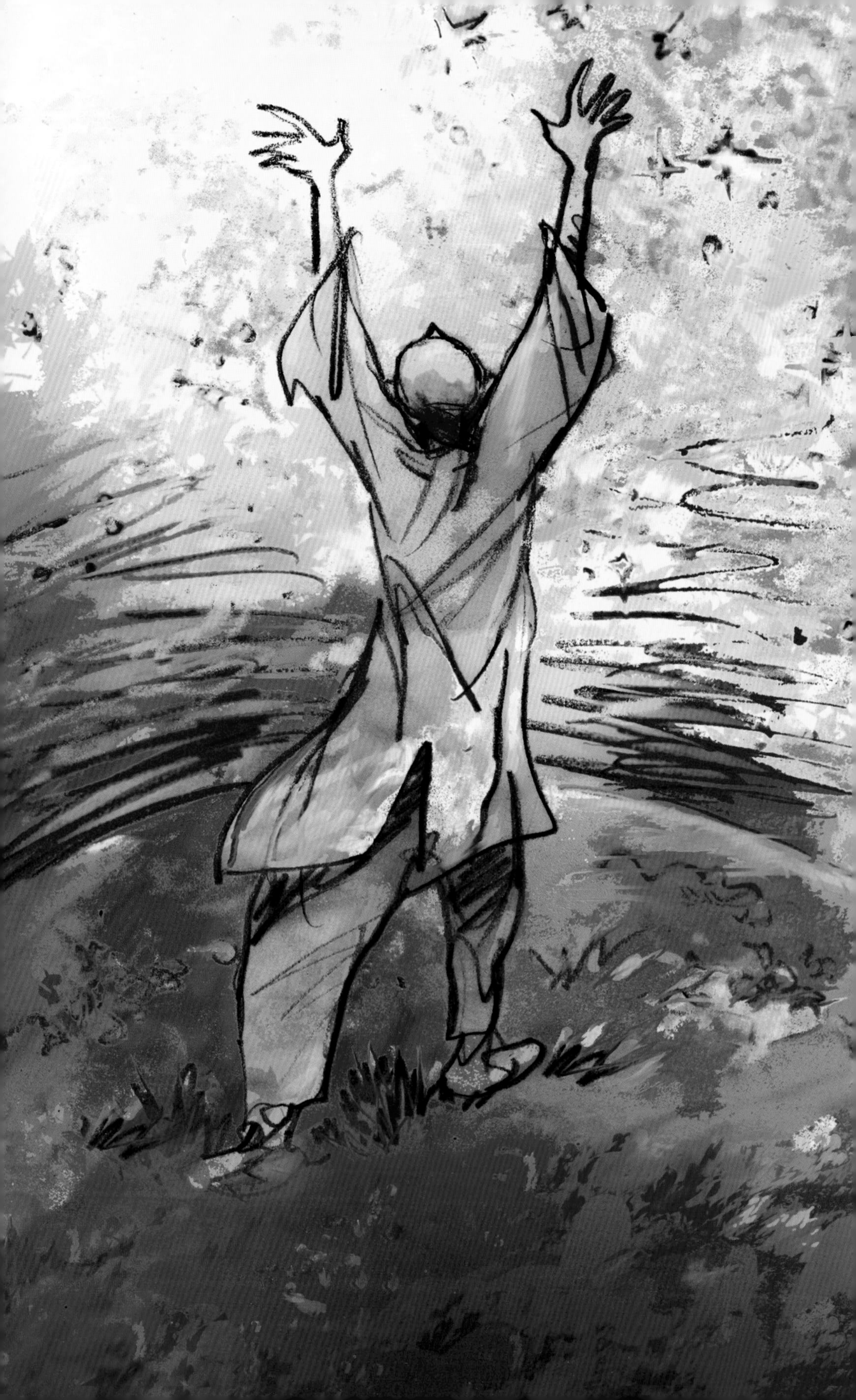

Part 2

Thanks

Tears of gratitude run down my face,
and that is my prayer.

Etty Hillesum

Thanks to the metal bell hanging from the branch
blackened by lightning

Thanks to the sound that runs through the countryside
suspending the world for a moment

Thanks to a breath to come back home
to a quality that is more important than anything
we were doing saying or thinking

Thanks to the forest
and its magic

to its extraordinary gift
of restoring harmony and joy

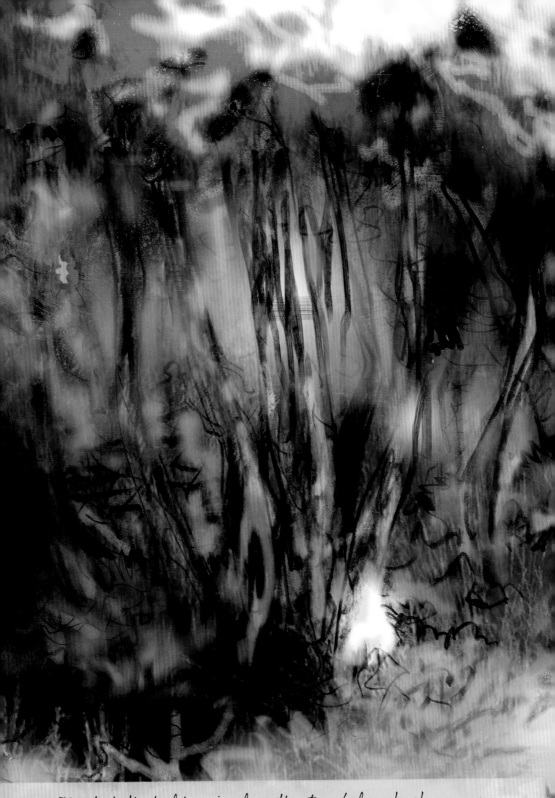

Thanks to the leaf hanging from the strand of a cobweb
        stretched between two trees in the distance
that suddenly   like an unexpected gift
        awakened me from the stories of my mind

Thanks to my spot

next to the big fallen oak tree

o the animals in the forest
which constantly amazed me

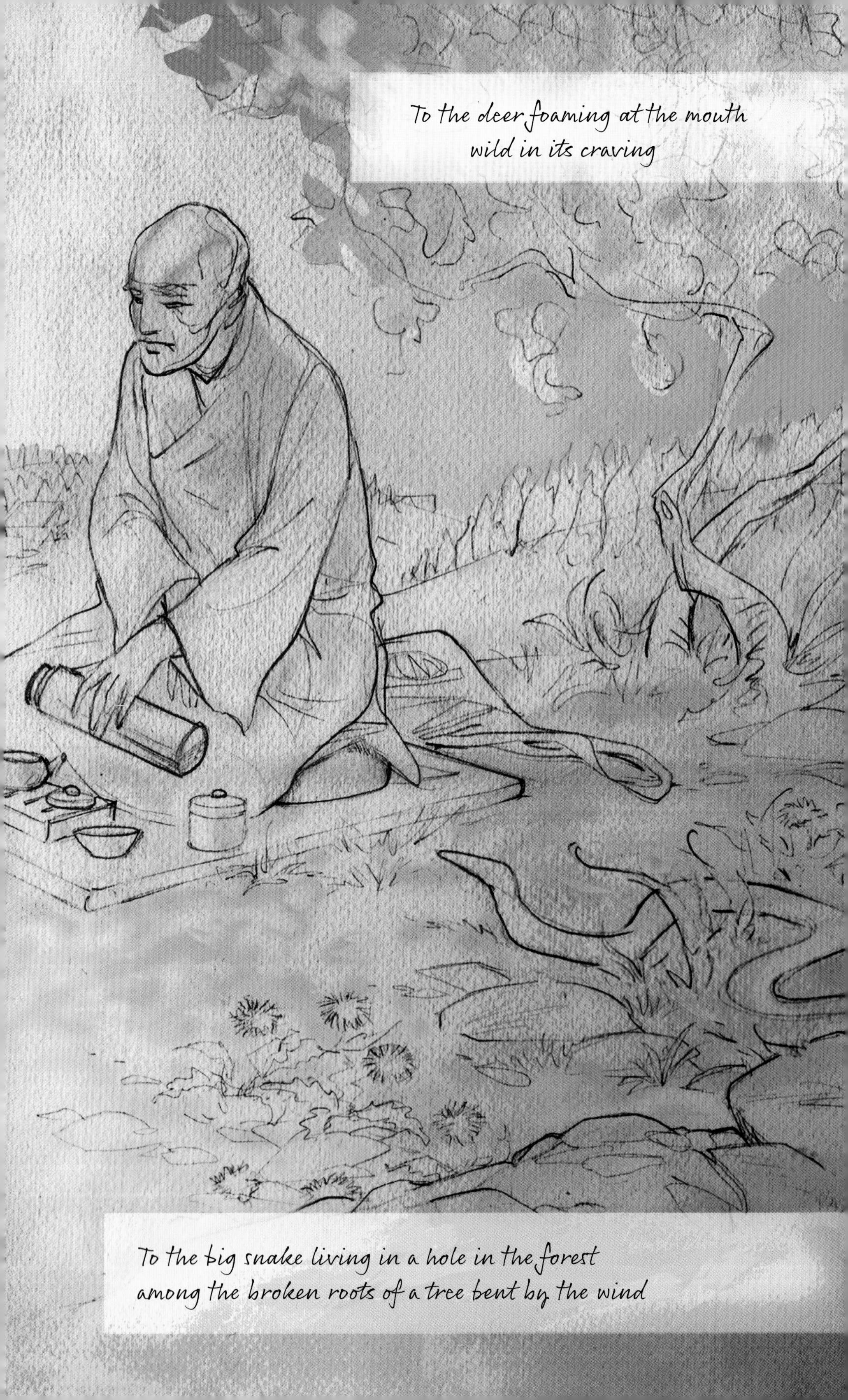
To the deer foaming at the mouth
wild in its craving
To the big snake living in a hole in the forest
among the broken roots of a tree bent by the wind

To the crows that would reply to each other
among the branches of the tall holm oaks

To the sun whose light would shine through
the branches to warm up my face

Thanks to the formal practice
and to its silence

through which the chatter of the restless mind
runs harmlessly

Thanks to the informal practice
to its simple joy and to its healing rest

Thanks to the perseverance and discipline of my sisters

To their silvery laughter
the sweetness of holding hands

and their joyful pride
in driving a tractor

The warmth of brotherhood during a break
to enjoy some tea   in the shadow of the elder tree

or in a hug

when life tests you

Thanks to the one who left at night leaving behind only
one robe   hanging on the wall
and after a cold winter in the Pyrenees came back

To my brother who knew how to find refuge
in front of the altar offering incense

or in a sunset down by the little pond surrounded
by the pine trees   solemn in front of a sky
splashed with intense red and orange hues

To the nutty brother who threw himself in the pond
of the white water lilies one hot evening

and has reappeared in the village of a healing shaman
in the heart of Brazil to show me that it's possible
to grow even without a monastic robe

Thanks to the gardener brother and to his joy in the morning
in putting the vegetables from the garden on the kitchen table

Thanks to the friend who would invite me at dusk
for a long walk along the hills covered
with vineyards

Thanks to the brother
who would not let anyone   lock him up
           who could not give up his freedom

Thanks to the brother who would make bread with the same
care with which in his previous life
        he had heated electrons

Thanks to my young abbot
to his sweetness   to his strength
and to his sincere humility

And thanks to the man he is becoming
Between a goat and a hoe

And thanks to the laughter
to the joy of my young brothers   to playing at the end
of a long day of practice

while the sun goes down setting the sky on fire

Thanks for discovering together
with ever-renewed awe

in the heart of daily
repetitive actions

that reality can surpass
the wildest fantasy

Thanks to the flu and the fever
that melted the near and distant knots
in the heart

and gifted me with moments of
solitude
when I could
finally draw

letting the images
        tell me the most bizarre stories

Crazy stories where my past
                    my daily fears and hopes

would mix with the fairy tales
of fantastic characters

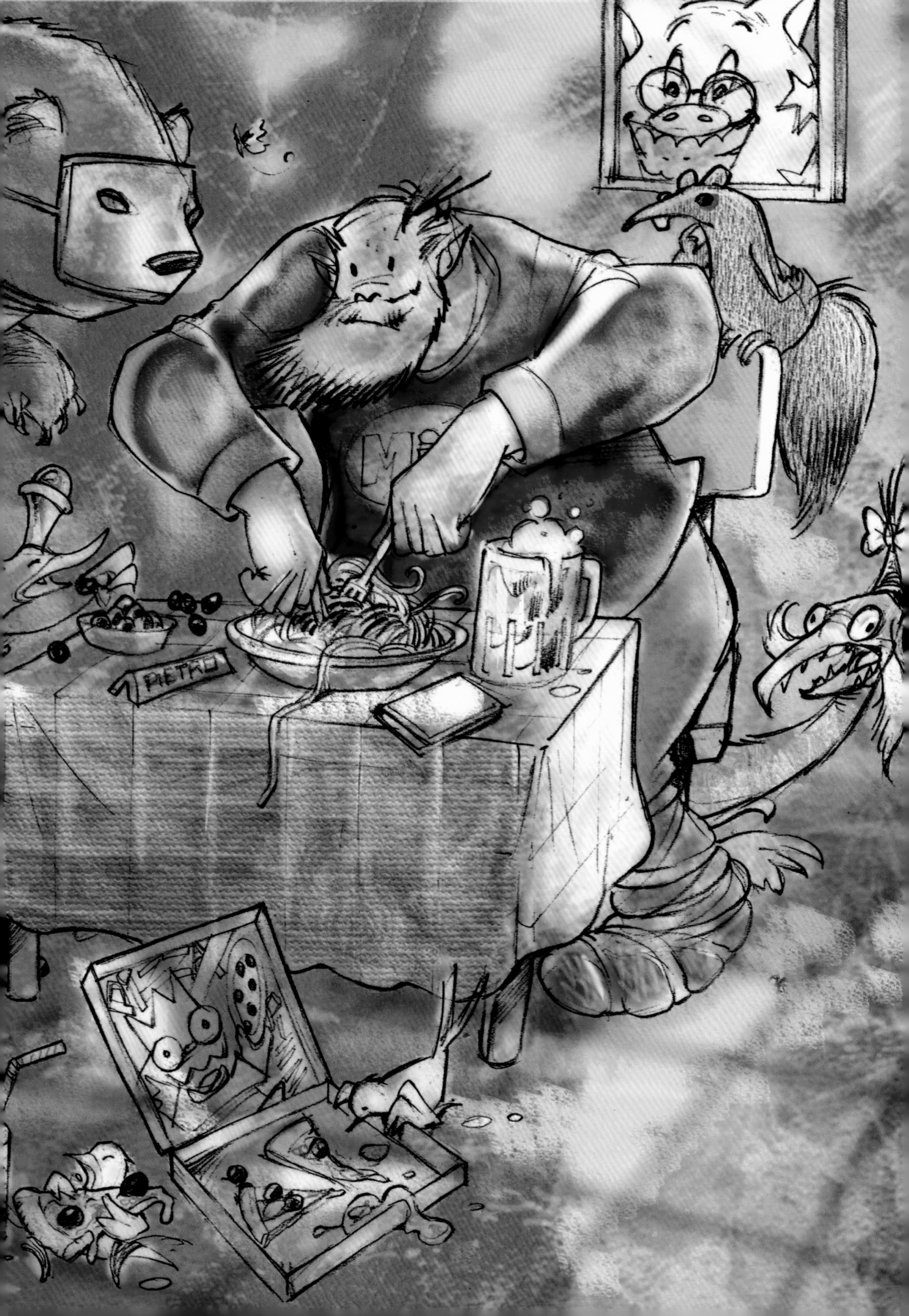
PIETRO

or of impossible journeys

where a poor monk would discover
he did not know how to love

or he would fight death

because
while taken by a thousand commitments and
worries
he had lost the deep meaning
of his choice

I had stopped for several years
and was surprised to discover that
not only had I not lost my ability to draw
but I had made a definite improvement

and most importantly I could unleash a roaring creati

This unexpected gift came
not from an abundance of stimuli
but from a healthy and purifying
fasting from images

Thanks to the morning when
left behind to guard the deserted village
I could finally dance   after so many years

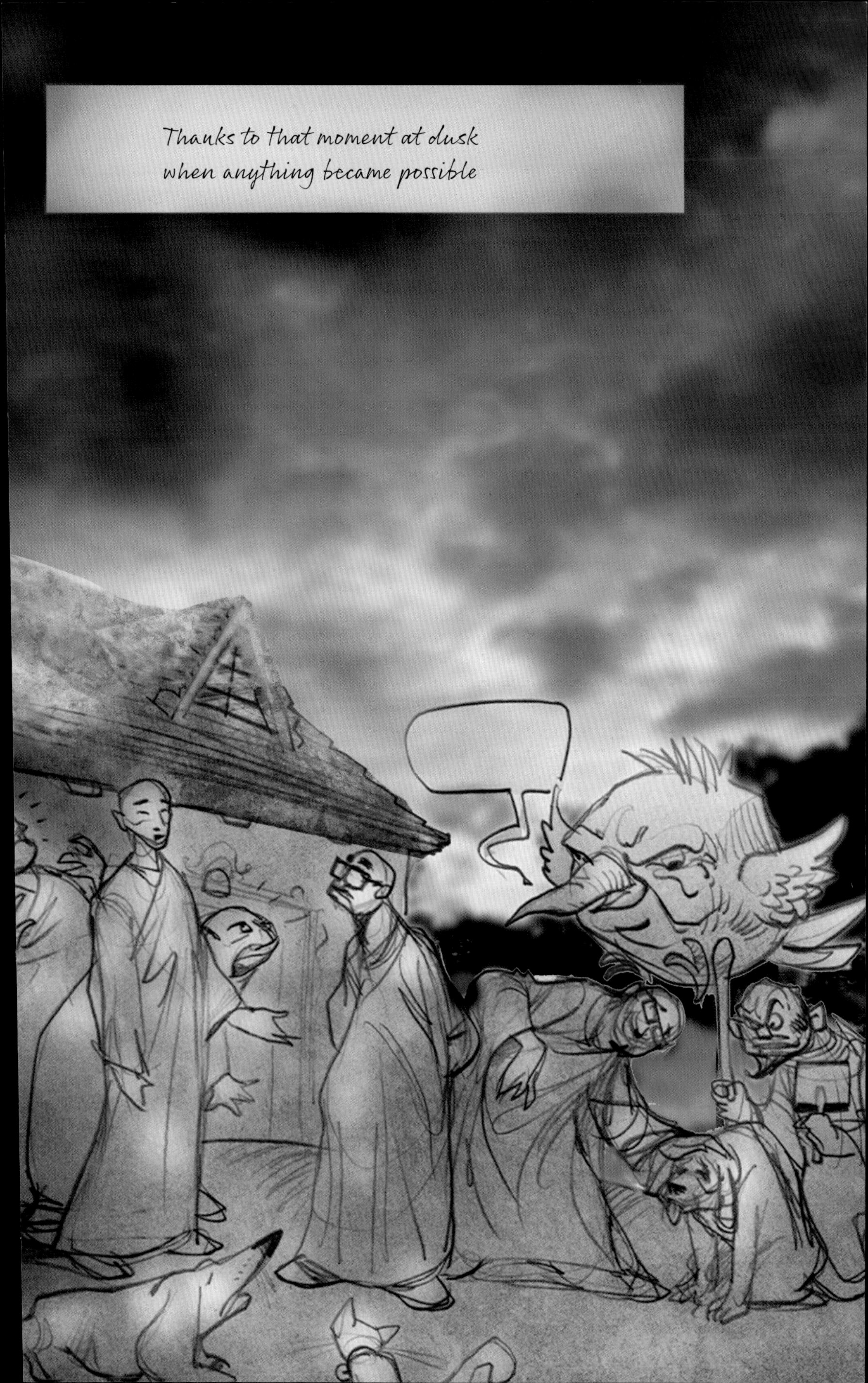
Thanks to that moment at dusk when anything became possible

Thanks to the hills covered with vineyards poplars sunflowers
to the magic rolls of hay placed by an artist god
over the threshed fields

To the distant fields that would become to my eyes
a sea that was not there

my sea

To the help that takes
the most unusual forms
at times the most unexpected ones

To the extended hand that I held on to and to the one
that I was not able to grab

Thanks for growing together
even though to truly open your heart you need time
and much   much courage

Thanks to the deer head hanging on the wall of a monastery
in the Pyrenees   for it explained to me something about death
about the beauty of having a little precious time to live

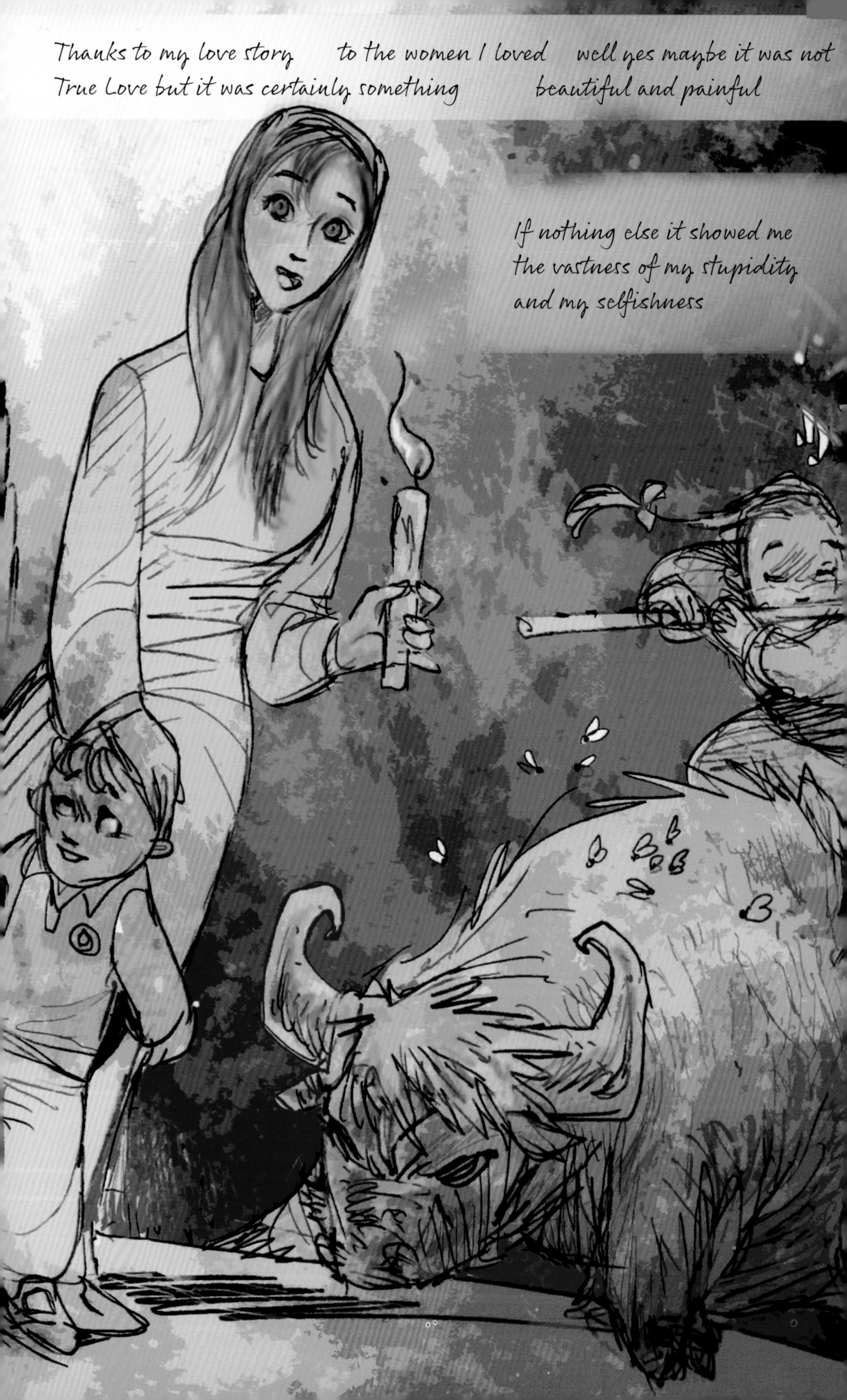
Thanks to my love story to the women I loved well yes maybe it was not True Love but it was certainly something beautiful and painful
If nothing else it showed me the vastness of my stupidity and my selfishness

Thanks to that hug
impossible and yet so wanted

the drought   the barrenness   that forces the roots of affection
to reach deep down in search of the well

Thanks to Sarvari who came to visit me with her parents

To remind me
of what I was giving up

Thanks to the shifts in the kitchen   thanks to the pot–washing
to the chanting and the bell that marked the rhythm of the day and the night
      thanks to the simple and humble chores
            thanks to the time devoted to study

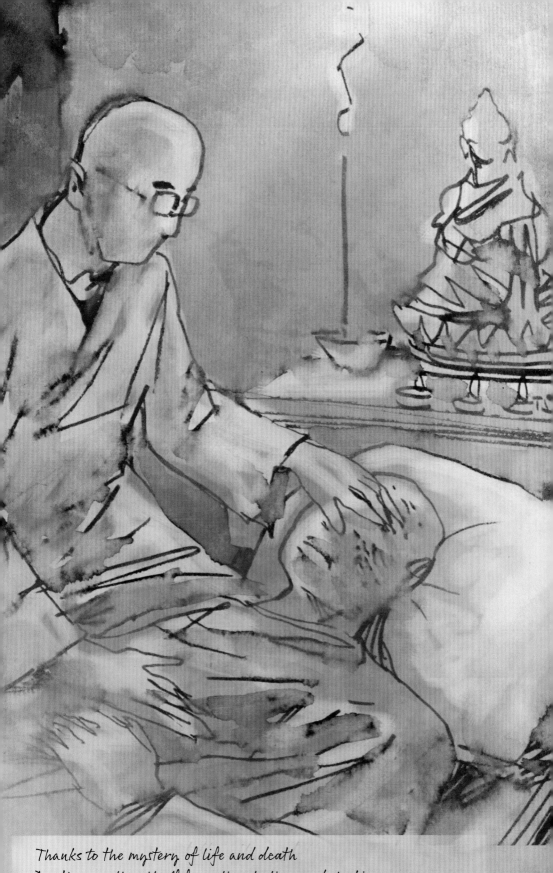

Thanks to the mystery of life and death
Death revealing itself from time to time and shaking us up

Thanks to desire that drives away
the arrogance of feeling special

Thanks to resentment   thanks to despair
to anger   to confusion   that helped me
not to believe all that the mind tells me

and in some fortunate cases
not to take myself too seriously

that taught me that I could breathe
and rest in the heart of the most intense emotion

To my brother who gave us his life
to awaken us from the illusion of perfection

Thanks to friends   those who
love you
and those who hold a grudge against you
and nobody knows why

It's all a beautiful game of mirrors
to help us understand how subtle
the distance between us and the other is

Thanks to solitude   so feared in the past
        and now become such a sweet friend

To the long ceremonies that have taught me patience
Thanks to repetition that helps me discover
that this moment is always new

Thanks to the tofu   to the pointed straw hat   to the foreign languages
with six accents that helped me discover the meaning of being different

In the bamboo forest the flock of starlings
dancing quickly into the sunset

They follow each other drawing
extraordinarily beautiful waves in the air
Who needs a miracle
before such a dance?

Thanks to the precious gift of ordination
so desired and yet so feared

Thanks to the man who simply
with the dignity of his presence
reminded me

that I no longer needed
to beg for love   acknowledgment
pleasure at all costs

Thanks to the teaching
simple   obvious
impossible to grasp

They would move like a majestic
mountain   with slow steps   that
looked as if they could stop time

Thanks to this ancient tradition
to this stream of men and women
who remind each other
that in life there is a mystery

The awakening from the illusion of separation
the illusion of having to beg or bite
for something nobody has ever taken away from us

Far too many entrenched castles each on top of a mountain
attacking each other and defending themselves
by hiding behind some ideology or religion

The end of fear

A love imposing no conditions

In short   a real big deal . . .

Thanks to the lack of creed   of ideologies
of affiliations
that allowed me to meet Jesus
his simple sweetness

his friendship
a friendship that once found can never be lost
the mystery of his forgiveness
for so long ignored   evaded

To that little church surrounded by a small cemetery
always open   protected by tall cypresses
and stone houses   deserted   narrow   among fields of sunflowers

Thanks to the one who planted those
plum trees overflowing with fruit
The slender cherry trees   the fig trees that
found their way between the blackberry bushes
to offer you their little dry fruit so sweet

Behind the buzzing of an insect
behind the distant hammering of a tractor
a river of silence thick profound
and real

A sip of it was enough
to end a long drought

Thanks to the Super Monks who do everything so nicely
They are good generous intelligent they play instruments and sing
they know how to cook and speak English and Vietnamese

while at night you dream of cheese
and struggle to even give up a marker

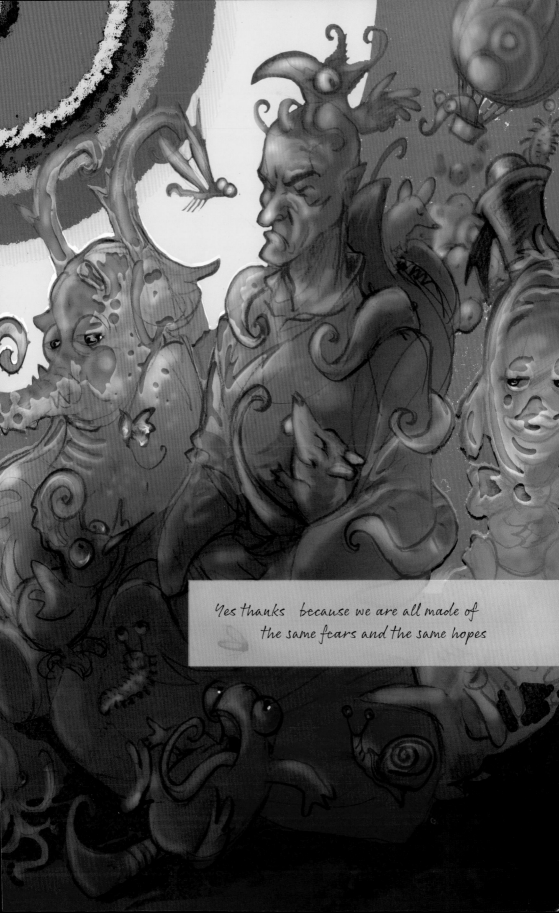

Yes thanks   because we are all made of
the same fears and the same hopes

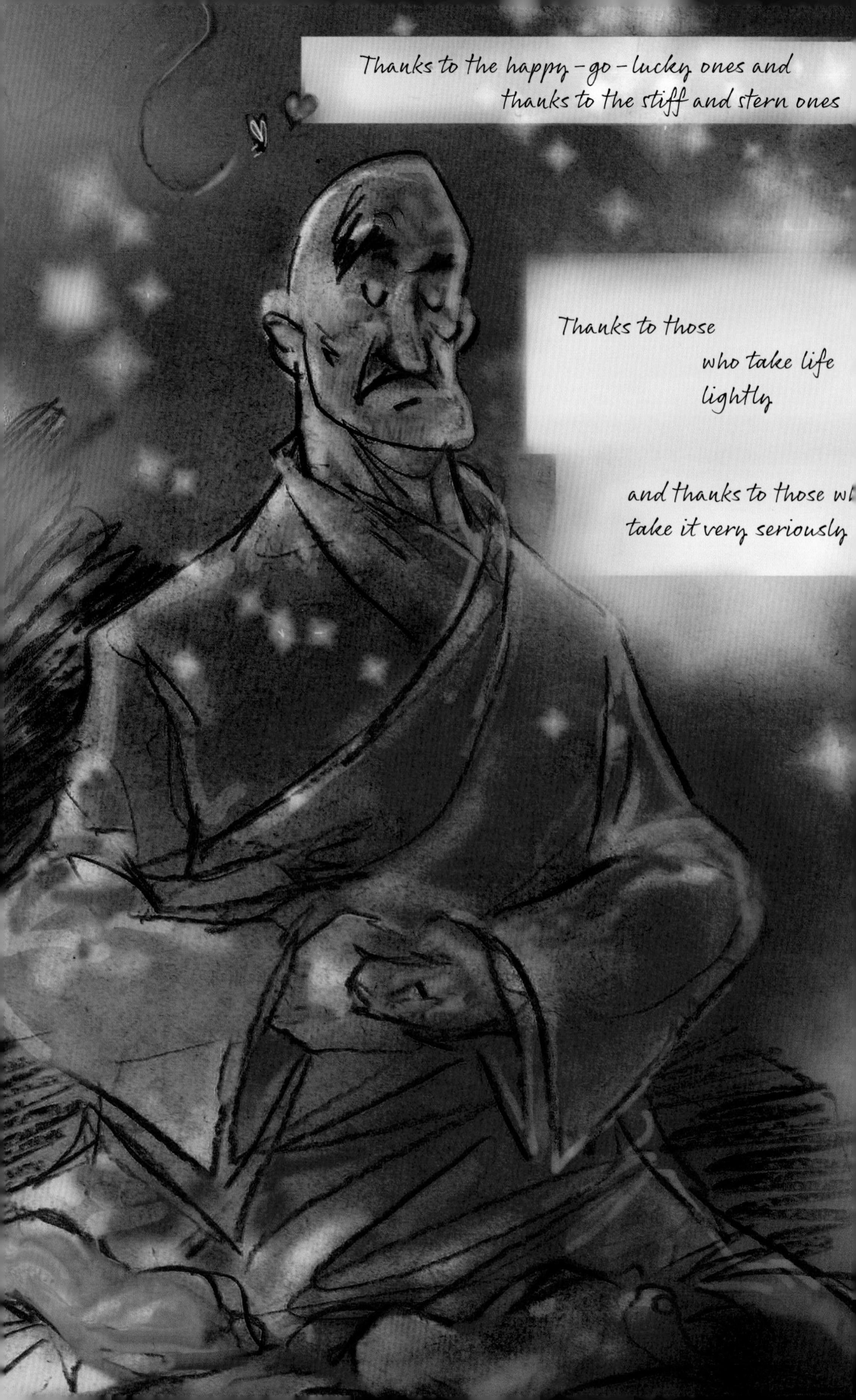
Thanks to the happy-go-lucky ones and thanks to the stiff and stern ones
Thanks to those who take life lightly
and thanks to those wh
take it very seriously

We remind each other
of the beauty
of a well-tuned guitar

Thanks to Martino who since he was
a little bean in the womb would take his mother to
meditate in a beautiful place

where you could see the lights
the sea and the big ships

where the loud screaming of the
seagulls would blend with the
distant sound of
the sirens of an ambulance

Thanks to Nina   shy   sweet
   smelling of rosemary and wet fur
To the distant undertow in the Salento moonlight

Those little yet great moments of joy that knew how
to melt away the sadness of an entire week

just like those signs you encounter while you follow
a path in an unknown forest
signs that tell you suddenly that you are headed
in the right direction   that you are not lost

Thanks to the strange courage of letting go of this
great love

to obey a greater
love
Even more simple and urgent
compelling   inevitable

Thanks also to the courage
of letting ancient pain emerge
of overcoming fear
of going through stifled emotions

Thanks to the monk and thanks to the wolf
may they walk together

Thanks to the new unhoped-for friendship
with myself
Thanks to the friends who
walk with and support me

in this strange and always new journey,
on this sort of big rollercoaster
and are able to love me still

Thanks to you and to all those
who don't burn their lives away by fleeing

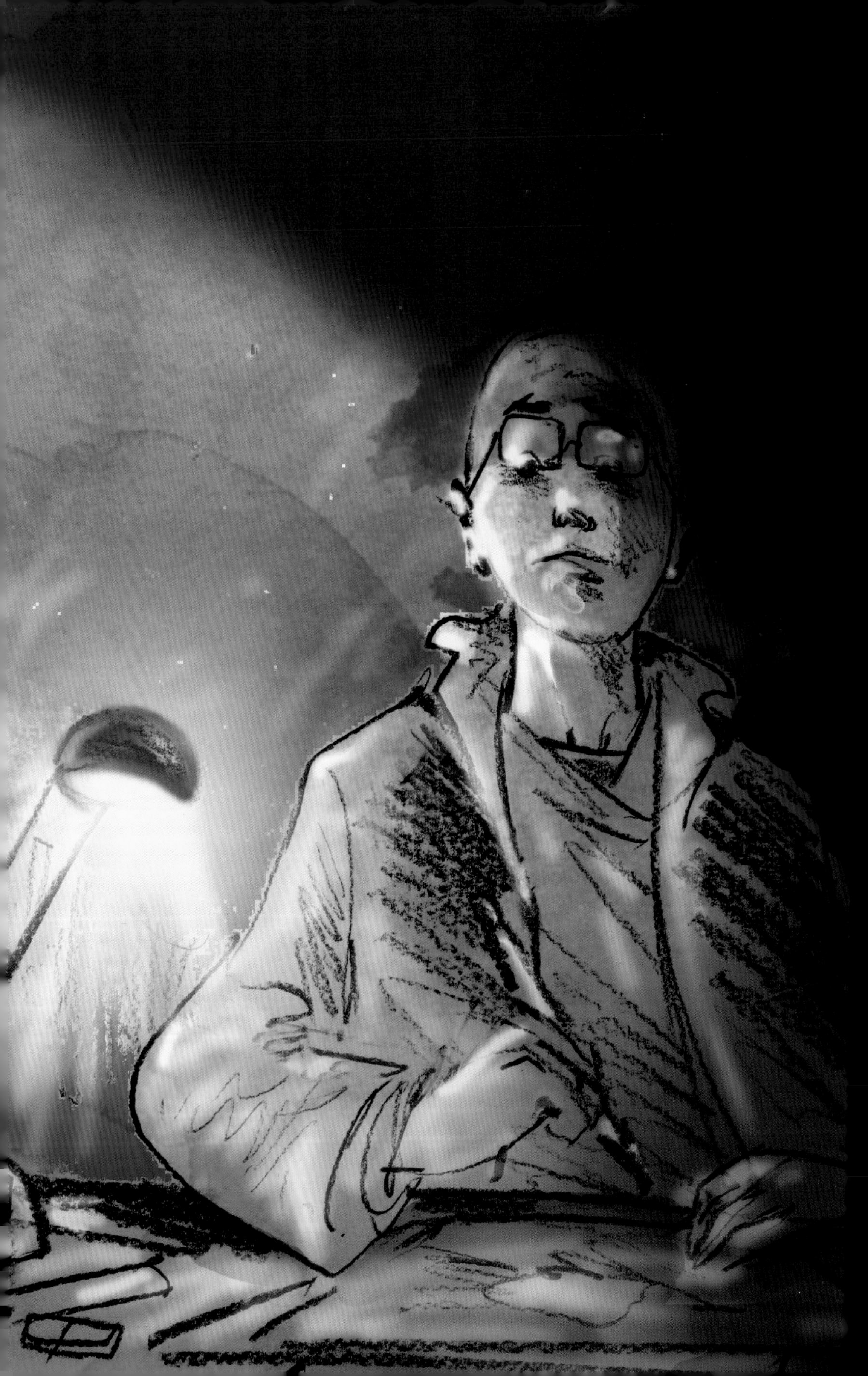

Gracias a la vida, que me ha dado tanto
Me ha dado la risa y me ha dado el llanto
Así yo distingo dicha de quebranto
Los dos materiales que forman mi canto
Y el canto de ustedes que es el mismo canto
Y el canto de todos que es mi propio canto

Violeta Parra

Thanks to life, for it has given me so much
It has given me laughter and it has given me tears
This is how I know the difference between happiness and heartbreak
The two elements that form my song
And your song, which is the same as mine
And everyone's song, which is the same as mine

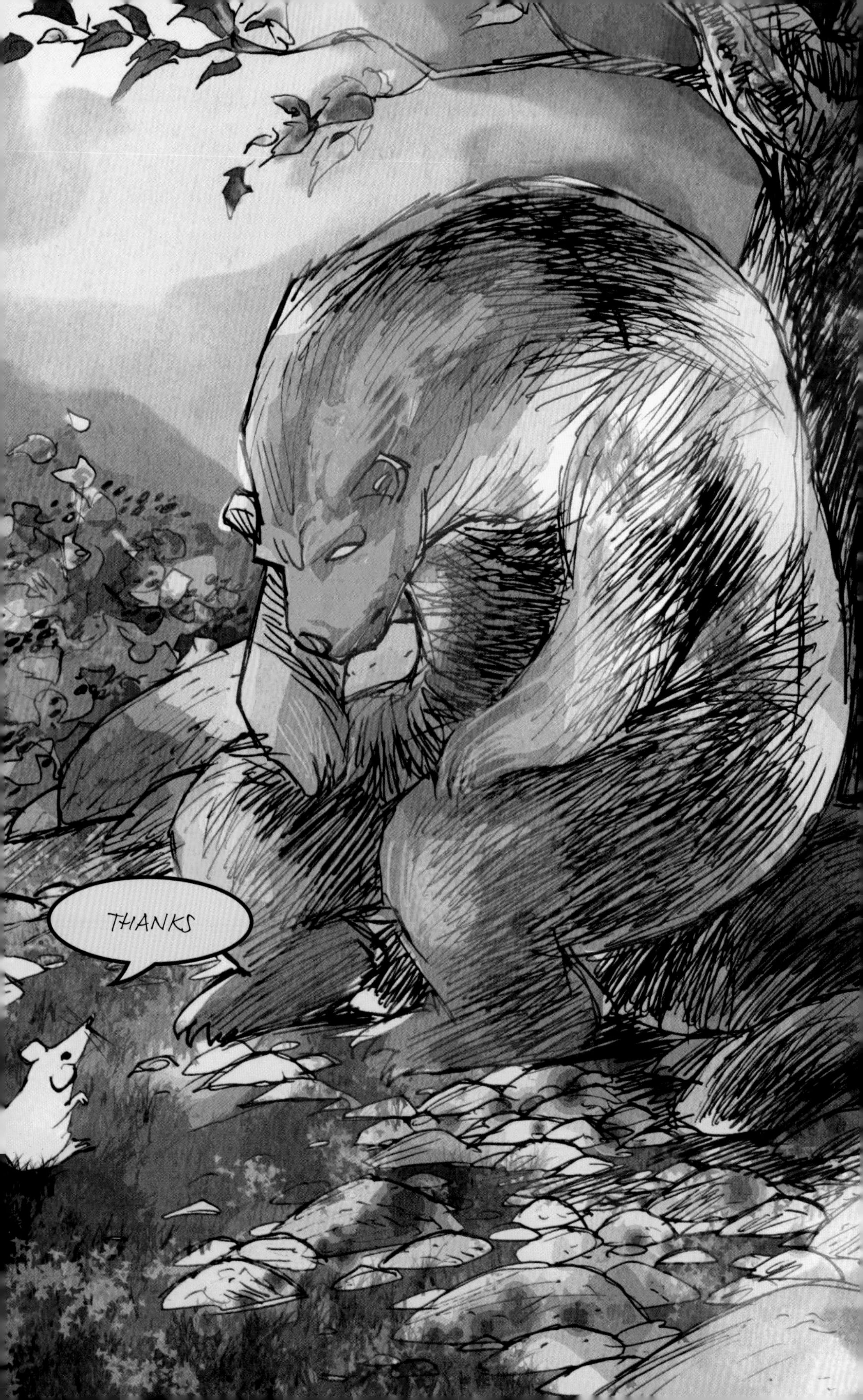
THANKS

An Imprint of MandalaEarth
PO Box 3088
San Rafael, CA 94912
www.MandalaEarth.com

 Find us on Facebook: www.facebook.com/MandalaEarth
 Follow us on Twitter: @MandalaEarth

Library of Congress Cataloging-in-Publication Data available.

ISBN: 978-1-68383-640-7

Publisher: Raoul Goff
Associate Publisher: Phillip Jones
Creative Director: Chrissy Kwasnik
Designer: Brooke McCullum
Editor: Tessa Murphy
Associate Managing Editor: Lauren LePera
Senior Production Editor: Rachel Anderson
Senior Production Manager: Greg Steffen
Production Associate: Eden Orlesky
Translators: Rossella Barry and Rita Melissano

ROOTS of PEACE   REPLANTED PAPER

Mandala Publishing, in association with Roots of Peace, will plant two trees
for each tree used in the manufacturing of this book. Roots of Peace is an
internationally renowned humanitarian organization dedicated to eradicating
land mines worldwide and converting war-torn lands into productive farms
and wildlife habitats. Roots of Peace will plant two million fruit and nut trees
in Afghanistan and provide farmers there with the skills and support necessary
for sustainable land use.

Manufactured in China by Insight Editions

10 9 8 7 6 5 4 3 2 1